Covers

TONY LOPEZ is the author of more than 20 books of poetry, fiction and criticism. His most recent poetry collections are *False Memory* (Salt, 2003) and *Devolution* (The Figures, 2000). He has received awards from The Wingate Foundation, The Society of Authors, and the Arts & Humanities Research Council. His poetry is featured in many anthologies including *Twentieth-Century British & Irish Poetry* (Oxford), *Vanishing Points* (Salt), *Other* (Wesleyan) and *Conductors of Chaos* (Picador). *Meaning Performance: Essays on Poetry* was published by Salt in 2006. He is well-known as a poetry performer and has given readings throughout UK, Europe and North America. He teaches in England at the University of Plymouth, where he was appointed the first Professor of Poetry in 2000.

Also by Tony Lopez

Poetry
   Equal Signs (Equipage, 2004)
   False Memory (Salt, 2003)
   Devolution (The Figures, 2000)
   Data Shadow (Reality Street, 2000)
   False Memory (The Figures, 1996)
   Negative Equity (Equipage, 1995)
   Stress Management (Boldface Press, 1994)
   A Theory of Surplus Labour (Curiously Strong, 1990)
   A Handbook of British Birds (Pig Press, 1982)
   Abstract & Delicious (Secret Books, 1982)
   Change (New London Pride, 1978)
   The English Disease (Skyline Press, 1978)
   Snapshots (Oasis Books, 1976)

Criticism
   Meaning Performance: Essays on Poetry (Salt, 2006)
   The Poetry of W. S. Graham (Edinburgh University
     Press, 1989)

Covers

Tony Lopez

CAMBRIDGE

PUBLISHED BY SALT PUBLISHING
PO Box 937, Great Wilbraham, Cambridge PDO CB21 5JX United Kingdom

First published 2007

Printed and bound in the United Kingdom by Biddles Ltd

Typeset in Swift 9.5 / 13

for Sara

ISBN 978 1 84471 338 7 hardback

Salt Publishing Ltd gratefully acknowledges
the financial assistance of Arts Council England

1 3 5 7 9 8 6 4 2

Contents

Acknowledgements

Some of the poems included here have previously appeared in the following publications: *The Alterran, Argotist Online, Free Verse, Jacket, Pilot, Poetry Review, Pog, Shearsman, Shiny, West Coast Line, April Eye: Poems for Peter Riley* (Infernal Methods), *Accomplices: Poems for Stephen Rodefer* (Equipage), *A Meeting for Douglas Oliver* (Infernal Methods/Street Editions/Poetical Histories), *Christopher Cook: Changing the Need* (Towner Art Gallery and Hirschl Fine Art), *Equal Signs* (Equipage), *Ezra Pound and Referentiality* (Presses d'Université de Paris Sorbonne), *Further Evidence of Nerves* (Cambridge Poetry Summit 2005) and in *Meaning Performance: Essays on Poetry* (Salt); I wish to acknowledge those publications and record my thanks to the editors and publishers concerned: David Dowker, Jeffrey Side, Jon Thompson, John Tranter, Matt Chambers, David Herd, Robert Potts, Jesse Seldess, Charles Alexander, Michael Friedman, Miriam Nichols, Peter Hughes, Rod Mengham, Tony Frazer, Peter Riley, Wendy Mulford, Nigel Wheale, Hélène Aji, Sara Crangle, Sam Ladkin and Chris Hamilton-Emery. 'Sequel Lines' was composed for a performance at 'Ezra Pound and the Twentieth Century' the 19th International Ezra Pound Conference, Université de Paris – Sorbonne (Paris IV) in July 2001 and is made entirely from research papers delivered there by Pound scholars. I am grateful to the organizing committee: Hélène Aji, Peter Nicholls, Jean-Michel Rabaté and Christine Savinel, for their generous hospitality and support. '1 Screen' and 'Z Screen' were commissioned by the Towner Art Gallery for a catalogue to accompany 'Christopher Cook: Changing the Need', a touring exhibition of the artist's graphites on paper and aluminium; thanks to Christopher Cook and to the curator Matthew Rowe. The talk poem 'Not Reading "After"' is freely transcribed from a performance at 'Total Writing London', Camden People's Theatre in June 2003, thanks to Chris Goode who organised the festival and to Tim Fletcher who made the recording.

I wish to acknowledge support from and record my grateful thanks to the Arts and Humanities Research Council for a research leave award, which enabled the composition of this work.

1 Screen

They stand before you in a light that comes from elsewhere
having no possible origin. Is this art history or mass immigration?
We can do unrelated facts, reconstructed contexts, lost aporias,
for we know well enough all these squadrons and arms dumps.
A van full of explosives parked close by a school—
then two small dogs join us in the graphics
as a site hosted by *Tripod* goes down the plughole.
Add 3. A full-fat blueberry muffin in "absolutely
incomprehensible", the latest makeover style. LEVEL 4.
Who threw the first stone? Who dug the foundation trench?
Shadows that never quite gave them a third dimension
were small, backlit, well-informed. *Clio, Twingo, XSara*
are the magic names that will be embedded in stucco
inside of the tree. If you need to make a claim
you write it out in longhand and blot the page.
I hear that Bush has decided to rat on Kyoto
and work on projects that would have otherwise
been impossible. Are we not all Palestinian?
Petals turn into butterflies, historical pipework,
a grey-green aperture in the middle ear. Ready or not.

& Far Away

On stalker's paths
asylum seekers
might just walk
the timber line
into the free end
where stealth bombers
and non-renewable
mental resources
known as snakeheads
the logical conclusion
snow-capped mountains
in hostile territory
a loss of tissue
beside the stream

Lights a fire
to find the way
old maps and books
grown in Albania
from these requirements
permissive paths
broken crystals
a piper's son
transported boulders
non-white migrants
smoothly uniform
zones of contention
or prefab huts
in blue-white light

And upland areas
with added butter
are worn away
in seeking to ensure
convention status
for boulders or trees
technically restrained
common-law rights
are not recorded
in direct sunlight
to transit camps
half-way across
this lovely peak
a suspect hold

For cloud shadows
set out to dry
on definitive maps
a question of money
becomes impassable
with growing dismay
carried in reserve
when he was young
these exit visas
into a safe country
more or less defined
who leaves on horseback
a public hearing
in melting snow

Black Panther Colouring Book

When the lights came back on, everybody looked like shit
Hardest hit was the airline industry

None of us even lives in New Cross
We are like vapours tossed into the nothingness of noise

He was pulled from a hole in the ground
Determined in case law and medical evidence

The very devil of artifice and administration
Now the Taiwanese have developed their own racing style

So that they could play 'the enemy' in exercises
Mostly standard issue British chirpiness

Eating grass on the long road north
The pacifist star sported zero bling

Saddam Hussein is a fan of Hemingway
Sometimes the stories overlap, just like dances

Always localised, and with different variations
Putting the rubbish out, taking their kids to MacDonald's

Anthrax letters ready to send off
At a hotel near Heathrow airport

She could even go outside and see the trees or whatever
I've played a bit on my solo albums

Yet inherent in each of us is a deep desire
The suction machine was too loud

Like finger-painting without the washing up
Which pumps oxygen to her starved brain

Steering also has been restored
In Hollywood there's simply no kissing

Whether or not such bribes were actually offered
almost no-one then worked on the land

They are intimidating everyone, not only women
Creeping on hands and knees through matted thorns

And that was a good experience, when I was dancing
In the vilest conceivable way

Screening the film to executives, Cher and Demi were told
That it would be more fun to torture them

In a rough part of town
Based on familiar experiences like travelling

A little spoonful of jam
The only member of the Klan killed by police

In the gold-coloured car from which the shot was fired
You have to recognise voting strength

Both of these claims proved false
In at least 35 countries

This normal boy in his sensible knitwear
This calm happy girl who isn't me

Holds radical views in an open and tolerant manner
Allowing federal agents to tap any phone

And sleep as I in childhood slept
In a damp house in the country all alone

Clear and Present Danger

Shot from a passing car, meanings attached
to the task of consumption

People of the village lost many trees
and were driven from their homes

You might remember coming up at Waterloo
a cutting table must be provided

With a few enigmatic phrases
the Globe Theatre was burned down

Most terrorism is small-scale
carried out by a handful of people

Death squads hunted down suspects
who melted into air, into thin air

A vernacular knowingness that informs
the Oklahoma city bombing

Served to increase popular sympathy
desire in the ordinary sense

Freeze-framed we recall trauma
sanctioned by the return of the forename

The world is closer than you think tonight
walking on gravel in steady rain

Equal Signs

Migratory paths
seem more solid
precisely because
of devoted sisters
restored to health
as contending forces
for this remapping
hadn't yet begun
the period in which
to borrow money
shimmering metals
infinitive phrases
under the table
where she continues
inscribed on the frame

Beyond these isles
he gets freaked out
by sheer diversity
a larger field
at the moment when
economic logic
with berries in it
can free this girl
symbolic capital
is full of noises
subtle and profound
in which any item
is a pathway into
the welfare state
a veil of allegory

Took possession of
a magic lantern
to bring about change
at the going down
in isolation
hoped to evade
many of these aspects
or stomach acids
could open the door
most lying slave
surprised the art world
with serrated edges
continues to evolve
this means of redress
from moment to moment

Never fully empirical
I want to suggest
a religious gloss
on the social text
was anti-comedic
the comeback king
contains vivid colour
was himself downloaded
between source and filter
to possess the land
without test explosions
the simplest hypothesis
a standing wave
all human emotion
a means by which

The nuclear family
freely interwoven
as a critical matrix
brought to the fore
from virtual testing
of strategic imbalance
fierce, moody, patient
complicit in slavery
altogether abandoned
secular parables
at the level of culture
behavioural data
is used to infer
non-random features
closed at one end

A shift in subject
the most visible product
was forced to watch
outside the window
each kind of feeder
whose interest is justice
needs to be needed
though they oppose it
push to flush
recover the rivals
inarguably marginal
diasporic peoples
always the others
attempt to defer
self-apprehension

Lines crossed out
a boat adrift
withholds new evidence
layered on white
as legitimation
for ordinary people
that might be lost
in compact fission
which clouded perceptions
of enterprise culture
whose contradictions
always already
the most prismatic
add deeper meanings
left unresolved

By human agency
out of the programme
at various intervals
hoped to evade
short-term winners
and yet because
in toxic gas
the sole foundation
fails to describe
the outside choice
so is she elided
as the land itself
reinforced harmonics
returns to buildings
so recently burned

All the accumulated
metaphysical terror
progresses no further
to shield him from
revisions and subversions
of collective action
has usefully clarified
microscopic variations
much less a period
a point of retreat
was what awakened
service information
in phrase space
and unconnected
carried most weight

Sounds and energies
during the course of
acute loneliness
does indeed fuse
revolution or death
gaps between segments
of hard finality
also by particular
scatological images
which sought relief
in transfer of aura
the scab drops off
white steamer gone
breakfast materials
disemployment

Imperative demands
didn't actually get
French and German models
for recent years
people in trailer camps
after the break-up
on wooden rollers
a cheap metal statue
was unobtainable
so she responded
after 25 years
in a foreign light
events as such
puzzled and offended
the default mode

Function defunct
by almost any measure
a figure unweaving
humanist purposes
might conceivably be
empty of content
they hang suspended
a mode of protest
calls into question
actual information
that no-one uses
nor were they able
such conscience seeks
a necklace of skulls
we need to remember

Precedes performance
lives without meaning
becoming a subject
that quickly cleared
having no stomach
we need to remember
even at the risk
freely composed
collective experience
tended to defer
a social body
adhering to words
recalling the 60s
before the emergence
of burning houses

Virtually complete
modifying phrases
a three-legged cat
would like to posit
that Boulder interview
in at least 2 ways
colouring spaces
significantly enlarged
a forest fire
she chanced upon
a dangerous concept
came fully formed
in empty jam jars
to denounce the evil
each in her own

Longer in exile
a ferocious capacity
will overthrow
models for behaviour
which haven't been shaped
by violent enforcement
disarticulated
an interior landscape
I happen to occupy
in psychic trauma
embellished or comprised
to enfold the consequences
was Ornette Coleman
chosen for adoption
with equal bluntness

That began to surface
in sensuous detail
on bilingual roadmaps
even more frequent
the texture dissolving
musical formality
suffused the painting
being pulled between
negative loyalties
have been issued
in title therefore
not identical to
retrospective denials
and more acutely
alters the key

In degree or kind
of scurrying figures
any one decade
at least partly reactive
exhibits the features
to outrace closure
and perish into
smaller communities
dimly apprehended
prepositional density
also to suggest
on contaminated land
drying in tubes
exchanged for money
out in the cold

Whenever it seems
non-formulaic
our development template
has always been
to make some room
for public demonstration
had little chance
of the whole people
much less evident
energies released
in order to feel
nearly invisible
social injustice
of being nowhere
the active resistance

It also stands
reinforced harmonics
technically restrained
between serrations
for social control
but actually enjoy
unswerving focus
most categorically
to maintain resonance
reject the implant
may have migrated
thus further enhancing
stockpile reliability
as the tongue rises
becomes an abstraction

Windswept pathos
unmistakably
the reader unquote
conceptual wrecking
and was excitedly
seeking asylum
or nano density
about forty houses
aged ten or under
the cold war average
look into the camera
stunned no longer
each of them booked
and partially healed
riding on a train

Without any notice
the charcoal stays lit
supporting this boycott
put beyond use
in the rear studio
moderately priced
to allow his actors
the feel of the street
will be infected
as voting approaches
from anchors to zinc
the blizzard descended
trying to disarm
disinterested persons
who manage a website

It might go cheaper
on 52 compounds
to fend for yourselves
later this week
farmers are history
powerless and downtrodden
from coast to coast
whenever we needed
scenic riverfronts
upscale weddings
big timber companies
declined to submit
simple misunderstanding
is actually composed
by certified instructors

Some reaction shots
had to be cancelled
by natural means
and water related
this personal appeal
on the smaller end
could not sink lower
to issue an order
trying to ensure
children who died
were stuck in the snow
and expert advice
more like a dealer
not based on fact
and internal pressure

Exhibits the features
to keep and bear arms
missing the point
and enjoy this too
no other institution
could lie ahead
a network of trails
less than 20 percent
intercut with shots
the act expressly states
billions of particles
found lower crash figures
of human experience
this variable rate
and caused indignation

Tries to impress
too many lobsters
by technical design
had softened his stance
if symptoms persist
as a reminder
on a day labour basis
not arguing that
to kill bald eagles
a vulgar collective
washed and drained
all of Arcadia
welcome back, Bob
sand in his eyebrows
small pieces of coal

Out in the desert
demilitarisation
opened the way
for humans and animals
did not participate
each export model
over the disparate
cheers of the workforce
throughout the hearing
were later deleted
actuarially reduced
injured and bereaved
being more numerous
seen laughing together
will not come cheap

Using reasonable force
the party leader
gives accurate readings
and sees no limit
with less to live on
using the software
would enhance air safety
an over reaction
important to stress
for so many critics
are lightly armed
with bits of speech
that very day
shown on TV news
is actually framed

A special girl
had parted company
when violence broke
is over the limit
for retention of organs
unreliable forecasts
of your choice
a rush-hour express
the needs of users
unloaded its cargo
of absolute nonsense
on an ordinary day
to get more soldiers
and announce their presence
on commercial stations

Who seemed reluctant
to restore wetlands
open to anyone
denied a request
to be reintegrated
fighting the blaze
becomes too intense
by leaving Africa
that voting segment
announces their presence
open to anyone
needing special care
is easy to imagine
the copyright symbol
in several poor countries

A holding company
hit separate targets
tested and replaced
technological solutions
quarried by slaves
could have been ruined
by these interruptions
safer for biking
assembly line workers
have vigorously denied
procedural problems
more diffuse networks
painted on canvas
millions of cars
beyond the perimeter

In Photographs

A pair of Iranian twins joined at the head
far from settling this increasingly bitter row
swiftly and grimly appeared to transmit the story
because it had been in the public interest
an inquiry into the good faith of one man
from Hereford to London misrepresented the situation
when an express train hit a transit van
the politics was driving the intelligence
when an express train hit a transit van
let me tell you how the scores have changed
possibly pronounced 'STROOD' as far as I know
three people, believed to be fruit pickers, died
and may have been acting in good faith
although we were divided on that issue but otherwise
supporters of the gay priest now not-to-be Bishop of Reading
Iraqis provide information about attacks on Americans
the veracity and honesty of our government
I wondered whether that was worth saying
whether or not the claim was well grounded, well founded, I mean
either a cow or a woman with a cow's horns
became prime minister in 1958 and was assassinated
back in apartheid days
Mr Straw calls for an apology from the BBC
let me tell you how the scores have changed
fourteen to Mr Good
this long-range ballistic missile travels 800 miles
without seeing the actual documents
about whom we know nothing
nor do we know his motive on the basis of evidence
whether there was undue pressure
and where exactly is Kim Bauer now?
if the claim was not well founded
chemical or biological weapons could be launched

whether politics was driving the intelligence
which he had typed up on a very long roll of paper
taken from the foreign affairs select committee
in a transit van: a clear and present threat
needed to be established or not
and the evidence was to the contrary
that the 45 minute claim
could have been avoided
and the people were misled and the parliament was misled
denied access to witnesses
about whom we know nothing
and Jack Straw hangs by his thumbs then passes out
tries to pull the rip-cord but passes out
is shocked by a security man rogue element
falling on a dodgy dossier, he passes out
he looks worn out but handsome in Arab dress
they hang him up again by the thumbs
and he is interrogated by Robin Cook
who wants to know about allegations made
by a gay priest from Reading called Elizabeth Bishop
whether politics was driving the intelligence
making this 45 minute speech
or whether it was in fact a sky-dive
a man addicted to risk
making a complete *Horlicks*
falling out of the sky
but acting in good faith
like a certain celibate not-to-be Bishop
serving on the joint intelligence committee
and not the other way around
Mr Bauer called for an apology between 2 AM and 3 AM
when the bomb went off in the desert
as far as possible from Los Angeles: maybe Phoenix

maybe Tucson, maybe Bazra, maybe Janin
the verdict NOT PROVEN
I wondered whether it was worth saying
whether or not the claim was well founded
how much it would cost to get a bulldozer
how much should I allow on the arts council application form?
what would be the appropriate delivery system
to get it over the level crossing
and into the settlements in good faith?

Late Works

Let us now, in order that we may clear the way, seek out what remains of the Italianate mood. Best of all we like art gossip, since the language we call illustrious can be neither approved nor denied. The pure despise alliteration, but who wants to be pure? Classic style was never before so simple and accessible. Both parts of the submission should be neatly typed and thrown into the air: a trace of pluralism should remain. I might wish that my days be bound each to each in level frequency, much the same as one another, but quite pleasant nonetheless. This form of irony has indistinct limitations. Try to avoid premature naturalisation. All crises are subject to weather, tide and local conditions: at the end of the footpath is a rustic seat and a rural cot. *Clematis montana* on red brick. The little signpost says *Members Only*. Since we have no guns we throw stones and whatever rubble can be picked up, making sure we are on camera.

Look at how the passing of time is erased in the story. Because of engineering works on the line, a bus service was used to ferry passengers beyond the section that was being worked upon. But our ticket was transregional, and so the instruction did not apply to us, nor contained within it even any remote cultural memory of the sabbath. Tanks began moving through the streets. What became of tankies (I mean hard-liners) when the wall was pulled down? By now they are all looking at pretexts that might provoke constructive dismissal with enhanced pension rights. Life membership of the *National Trust*, serviced leasehold apartments: you will need to pay tax on benefits in kind. This was Britain in the late nineties. The language used by a given individual immediately indicated a political position, and no neutral or objective alternative was available. Who *was* Harriet Harman?

A picture held us captive and our friends were transformed into plot-ciphers, moulded in aluminium for high definition and ease of assembly. If you're not happy with any passage you read, we'll quite simply replace it or refocus your attention without question. This is what we call intellectual property. Have you, by the way, considered a career in human capital transfer? Sign here to confirm that you are available and actively seeking money-off coupons. No-one listens to poetry, but there are lots of other ways we can deliver on quality. Each voucher is valid for a separate two-week period, so you can enjoy savings in permanent black ink. Individual identity is expressed in customized paintwork, total-body spray jobs, and intimate tattoos. The herald might be a mentor or an enemy at the moment of the call. Imagine this is such a moment.

The lyric may now be brushed clean and inspected. It should be perfectly straight and the turns rounded. Check the welded ends carefully for cracks and ambiguities. As with figures of negation and other load-bearing structures, all allusions must be in perfect condition. Renew suspect or bent words immediately. The refitting procedure is simply the reversal of that for removal. Referential meaning is superfluous but always breaking into the semantic horizon. Take care to use new self-locking stops, sprung commas and semicolons as appropriate. Tighten paragraphs to the torques specified at the beginning of this chapter, when the whole assembly has been lowered to the ground. A book should thus articulate about the spine depending upon the quality of your hyperbole, and furthermore it is the ambient temperature that will guarantee effective use over time. Binding glue is sensitive and becomes brittle when frozen. Let us therefore put our faith in interpretative communities and by all means give them something with which they may keep themselves occupied for many years to come.

Look at the Screen

Try 'art is history' remember 'Art is just a guy's name'.
Do we need quotation marks? Boarding passes? Transit visas?
The wall runs from the thruway down into a pond
then goes up the hillside, zigzagging some trees
already established.
A wall to look at and photograph
not a boundary or contested site: an Art wall.

Rubble in news photos—walls coming down in 1989 Berlin.
Notes for a power-point presentation?

Bulldozers going to Janin in 2002.

Remember Rock Hudson, much reduced, on the stretcher.
Was he the first big name to die of AIDS?

Clearing stones from a field you establish a boundary
working with the material that is to hand.
If you are dispossessed you fight with stones
or whatever you can pick up.

When Douglas Sirk employed deep focus lenses
expanding the field from canopy to roadside and gardens
in a pretty suburb, leaves fell across the view
building up a social meaning.

And in this scenario Rock Hudson reads Thoreau
runs a nursery, wears a check lumberjack shirt:
you keep trying the stones and taper towards the top
capping stone. Melodrama, Country Life,
A film called *All that Heaven Allows*.

Driving down the Taconic parkway in the fall
miles and miles of road-killed deer.
It's not about the ending: trite, cut-off, contrived:
turn and drive west across the Hudson river
imagine this is real life.

Not Reading 'After'

I'm going to ask you to help me this evening. What I want to accomplish between us is to imagine a poem that is already written, to try to invoke this poem without reading it, if that is possible. I've been thinking about this through the day, having been very moved by what's happened so far. The readings against the war, against the bombing in Iraq, leave me wanting to add a talk poem here, rather than another reading. And I could try to do that now by imagining an absent poem. I've been thinking about the beautiful elegy that Andrew Brewerton read for Doug Oliver. Listening to that reading and others, I've been remembering Douglas Oliver's book *In the Cave of Suicession*, which he wrote as a final BA dissertation project when he was a student at Essex University. There was an official procedure to apply for research expenses for the project. I understand that he claimed for travel and supplies: a cake, a sacrificial cake, a bottle of beer, crisps and so on, and he went to a cave in the Derbyshire Peak District to write his dissertation. He wrote that he drove to Winnat's Pass in 'his beige Austin car', put up a tent and went into the cave (an abandoned lead mine called Suicide Cave) and in his own quirky English (Scottish) apparently good-uncle style, he confronted the idea of the oracle, of another intelligence beyond conscious control, and of fear itself. I mean he tried to make his book open to that intelligence, fact or fiction; all his work was about that so far as I can see, even the most political writing. In my copy he wrote 'a pathway blasts out from this consciousness'.

In that book he goes beyond anything reasonable or sensible and the cave speaks, the genius of the place speaks, sometimes it's a bee, and the book, which is called *In the Cave of Suicession*, is of course a poem about suicide, about the fascination of death, that doesn't really talk about suicide throughout. It's not Plath. 'A bee flew into the cave.' Come in. There are a couple of seats at the front here. So the poem that I wanted to imagine is a holocaust memorial poem called 'After'. It's a poem that was produced in a roundabout way. It seemed to me that if I talked about what happened in order to make the poem that would be something, a sort of negative. It would be like Rachel Whiteread's sculpture of a house that isn't a house but a moulded replica of the space inside the house: a composed negative. That seems particularly appropriate just now. The first thing, a motive, was a view, a landscape view downwards from a mountain to a valley edge and some kind of habitation. But this view was not a view I saw in nature, it was a view that I saw in a picture in RISD (Rhode Island School of Design) gallery. I was in Providence because I was doing a reading having been invited there by Rosmarie and Keith Waldrop and they very generously put me up for a few days, so I had time to be a tourist in Rhode Island and I was feeling a long way from home of course (which was the point). I went to the RISD museum and there was an exhibition, a series of prints by a Japanese artist whose name I now forget, and they were all high mountain landscapes: the sense of vertigo and loneliness was particularly affecting, the attraction of the edge. So, Rosmarie and Keith put this party together for Maurice Scully and me and I had quite a bit to drink, I just slept for a couple of hours and then afterwards couldn't sleep at all. You get into this state where it's impossible to sleep and it happens more and more, so that the early phase of drunkenness gets shorter and shorter but when you wake up in the morning you're really spinning, there are lots of thoughts all at once and there isn't any structure to them it's very difficult. I was interested in using this state of confused clarity and hung-over craziness, so I started by remembering the emotion of the mountain picture and just wrote, pages and pages. The structure it fell into was quatrains with five words in each line. I produced maybe twenty pages without deliberate thinking, the writing was completely incomprehensible, a kind of nonsense, I was just seeing where it would go. I couldn't do anything with it at the time so I put that notebook away. Later on, about two years later on, I was in America again this time doing a tour right across and I became curious about this piece that had been written without the usual kind of motivation and control. At each place I stopped I was looking at this piece and wondering what I would do with it, would I read it or perform some of it? I started at a quarter past, they told me to use 25 minutes.

So anyway I had this piece of work that wasn't really usable but I knew that it was in some as yet private way important to me and I couldn't do anything about it and I probably would have forgotten it forever and not thought about it but Oh yes: it's the story of Sophie Wessex that suddenly makes this seem important again. Do you remember Sophie of Wessex? Sophie is the woman who married Prince Edward and when she married Prince Edward she became Sophie, Duchess of Wessex, before that she was just an IT girl, a PR person wasn't she? She married Prince Edward and she became, if you remember the story, it came out that she was using her position as a royal in order to get work for her PR Company. She was selling the idea that you could have a party with royals. You could get these people who wanted profile and maybe Edward or another prince would come to the party. There was a feature where she was doing this pitch to an Arab Sheik and it turned out that the Sheik was actually a tabloid journalist, and she was saying to him 'I can get you Philip, I can get you Betty, you know who my husband is, we can do a deal here', and the fake Sheik wrote it all up and made a huge media story. It was in the Sunday newspapers and it was the biggest story of the time. The idea of a phoney Arab Sheik meeting this duchess who is married to a prince in a hotel is a wonderful parable it makes me think about what would be a genuine Sheik? What is genuine royalty? What does it mean? Recently William had a fancy dress party didn't he, all these people turned up in fancy dress to Windsor castle and somebody came over the wall. He was a comedy terrorist, and he wore a pink robe and a headdress. He was supposed to be an *al Qaeda* agent but he was a comedian, they let him in and then they had to do a security review on the royal family. So my point is that if you have a fake Sheik the whole idea of royalty collapses. There's a woman on film in my childhood, she sits on a throne in a church ceremony and they put a crown on her head: she's suddenly a real queen. There's a boy who gets to age twenty-one and he's a real prince, the Prince of Wales, Lord of the Isles and heir to the throne of the UK and Commonwealth, future leader of the Anglican Church. This woman running a PR company, face to face with an Arab Sheik and she's trying to sell him a party with her husband, or her mother in law, or some other royal. She's completely corrupt obviously, she's using her position for the cheapest kind of advantage, building up her business, but it's the Sheik who's the fake.

It was a long time after I published the poem 'After' that this story happened. I was at a conference about performance poetry. I was in the middle of a talk and I just didn't quite get to the Sophie Wessex story. I was talking about Tony Harrison for three or four minutes and someone official came in, told me I had overrun my fifteen-minute slot, and I just snapped it off. So there was something unresolved I had wanted to explore between the way that Tony Harrison used the skinheads in his video poem V, made fun of their ignorance, and the new genre of the Martyr video. The story that I couldn't get to about Sophie Wessex, something to do with the theatre of royalty, had become topical in another way. I was coming to the special combination of fancy dress with an army, helicopter gunships and tanks. So anyway the point of this was suicide bombers because in the same week that 'Sophie and the fake Sheik' was the main story in the news the other story I noticed was the first profile on a suicide bomber that I'd seen in the press. A suicide bomber and his relationship with his parents, how they were really proud of him and thought he was doing a good job. The genre we have yet to come to terms with is the Martyr home video. A video says 'Here I am, this is what I'm going to do, I'm doing it because I know god's will, I'm going to meet god in heaven, I'll get my reward there'. So the other story was about the suicide bombers, their motivation, and the society around them. I found out recently that 40% of the land of Palestine is inhabited by Israeli settlers and that the 60% remaining area is about the size of the Isle of Wight. It's almost exactly the same size as the Isle of Wight and there are a million and a half people on this piece of land. It seemed to me that what was happening was horrible and awful, completely understandable, but something that was bound to happen. So these people are surrounded and the new fence went up quite recently and tanks moved into Janin with bulldozers and started flattening the place. Somebody made a comparison on the news between what was happening in the ghetto in Warsaw and what's happening right now in Palestine. I think there is a kind of connection; I was wondering how I could actually read a holocaust memorial poem while this was going on. So I decided that I would-n't read the poem but I would talk about these ideas instead.

The poem is a holocaust poem in a special sense, it doesn't narrate anything really, doesn't retell that story. There are some minor references, hints about things like the heaps of belongings, stored gold and broken glass of Kristallnacht. I couldn't say anything directly about that. There are still some people who can write out of direct experience, and there is the assemblage of recorded testimonies in the Washington museum, which is really clear. So what I finally did with the impossible text was to run it through a programme and completely randomize it, to take it further beyond conscious control. I asked a colleague in computing to make a programme which would take the entire vocabulary set, select groups of four words and produce completely randomized stanzas that would each have four words and four lines. Each time the programme ran the text was reordered and I ran it hundreds of times so I generated a huge text it was a big book like *OED* or something enormous, and then I just put it in a box for a long time because I couldn't see how I could do anything with it. I know you can't get a machine to write something for you. Someone who read a version, a much shorter set, said they recognised the story of an affair in it and someone else said that there was a polar journey. So what I did was to read through the expanded text and select, just picking out the small residues that had a kind of sense, like ashes in the bottom of a big bonfire. Any stanza that had any sense in it at all that I could find I preserved and then out of those I selected again until I got to the poem published in *Devolution* which is three or four pages long. Finding, selecting and arranging composed it. It doesn't have any narrative but it does have a kind of remote connection with the original piece that I wrote in Providence and it seems to me now to be an abstract poem I couldn't have made in any other way.

Sequel Lines

A memoir of childhood
and its libretto
is what I would call
lethal hysteria
normal circumstances
frankly contradicted
a subway map
superimposed
in 1944
can only repeat
designating Ovid
together in fact
technological warfare
beyond literal devices
across the surface

Explicitly composed
a schematic reduction
must be plotted
at the very least
preserves naively
tiresome melodiousness
guarantees immunity
that Guido recognises
the second meaning
original black
managed to vaporize
country and western
up to that point
aggressively blurs
the number eleven

A radio crowd
should underwrite loans
that multiply in
is not optimistic
you have the radicals
split open garbage
the medical tent
cannot be explained
performative tautology
hillbilly music
in other words
tends towards elegy
deluding himself
continues to follow
any set system

Tearing apart
contemporary idiom
turning as it does
in the market place
canto 90 for instance
the people the many
a brilliant sentence
tends to become
the structural centre
cannot erase
40 million Italians
in the same volume
a cemetery anecdote
the very noise
a falling away

In order to occupy
how they make obvious
this stage continues
a nomadic economy
did more to enliven
autonomous subjects
regular programming
which opens up
obstructions to learning
alongside the usual
luminous details
were very narrow
and resigned himself
three mixed sets
of ordinary people

This stage continues
reading for power
significant changes
we do not believe
an officer's tent
more overdetermined
reached page 51
that weightless feeling
deeper in fact
pieces of dynamite
hammering scansion
delusions of presence
might be translated
extensive and various
the noise they make

Between for instance
fails to palliate
a particular fantasy
was not the arena
of natural justice
documentary scraps
at the end of summer
driving down a road
the Mussolini opening
stays in the memory
a kind of presence
the fish itself
imagines her singing
undiminished political
dazzling surface

Irretrievably lost
a graduate student
in Natalie's garden
has more consequence
broken apparently
unable to clarify
military meaning
has been commended
into my mouth
effectively indicates
the greater abstraction
teeming with cattle thieves
much less coherent
citational strategy
does not erase

Generally speaking
historical urgency
can't really hold
material evidence
a passing siren
readily available
works to subsume
the ongoing text
on behalf of the masses
we hope to recognise
Florentine gangsters
and in particular
strong mountain wheat
in that respect
what reading is

By tacitly claiming
localised fidelity
deliberately blocked
no real significance
appears in exchange
calling into question
phobic intensity
we factor in
actual persons and places
little by little
contradictory stories
nailing his coat-tails
merely because
Kashmiri house-boats
on any inherent

The act of looking
erases significance
as if in a diary
thick black lines
by exfoliation
of 391
profoundly seditious
I'll try to suggest
three propositions
into this tent
or emotional drama
can thus appear
in a smoky light
commodity fetish
prosodic rent

Signs or tokens
freely articulated
to offer resistance
replaced by leather
and this in turn
Virginia etcetera
manages to recover
in lightning flashes
of numismatics
afflicted by presence
now undertook to
for condensation
can evoke the war
this much shorter
could not exist

These two projects
a kind of marvellous
if you have cancer
provides some evidence
persona must venture
of this resistance
when he has to choose
a deep anxiety
radically altered
the elite machine
is pieced together
body and voice
intuitive stagger
in *The Cantos* I think
what is emerging

Almost as though
the veiling of power
actually attributed
Nevsky cake shops
all but unreadable
imagines her singing
a mere two years
does not erase
the melancholy undertone
of silent comedy
even in England
progressively dark
if you could get him
a kind of remainder
for simple answers

Lifting belly
numerous replicas
the arcades material
often telephoned in
as he was typing
unrelated details
success to Marconi
three weeks later
at UCLA
night dogs howling
to be adjusted
the unified subject
was out of a job
a post-war moment
green and brown

Names read out
are sex-obsessed
speak for themselves
become small ringlets
the edge of resection
returns to Manhattan
in velvet trousers
an unfolding sentence
the yearly tribute
of externalization
this brief aria
holding together
spongers or admirers
never rely on
the radio dial

Before the collapse
on turtle stump
mechanical evidence
careful to isolate
the Cimmerian lands
contaminated with
backwards Romanticism
owned by an actress
torn from history
more anecdotal
we often forget
an implicit hierarchy
comes after the ruins
hopes and delusions
only one shot

Writing in exile
designedly loosens
unrelieved flimsiness
in that respect
seeming translucence
old currency ratios
first introduced
vertical strokes
functioning memory
can thus appear
highly elliptical
in the new sequence
prior to detention
fundamentally differs
in touch with things

Suddenly unable
we cut the tops off
his first impulse
has pencilled in
excellent sausage
significantly altered
traditional lyric
was routinely issued
to abolish complexity
both texts unfinished
the chocolate grinder
disappeared from the world
of consecutive numbers
and thereby authorized
monetary systems

Belligerent abstraction
discovering itself
variously reflected
the plural of table
attempts to evoke
in utopian writings
notoriously unstable
between scansion and money
a bitter recognition
to avoid each other
will further consider
his rival in Venice
a future in which
random permutation
is always already

The line grows thick
says Barbara Hepworth
a moment to come
would end arbitrarily
any new quality
extensive and various
saving the world
whose very movement
breaks and ruptures
technological warfare
alerting the reader
for thinking coherence
radical simplicity
foldable nearness
by and for love

A polemical book
shaped by criteria
to be translated
never fulfils
the light of recurrence
by her designs
for the premodern
of ethical nature
hopelessly retro
film keeps jumping
different typewriters
radioactive traces
who are initiated
unconnected fragments
scrapping in a bag

Ready to turn
the use of stone
to be invented
hidden and violent
clues are implicit
from the conviction
might offer or allow
the idea of paradise
our later perspective
gradually abandoned
feminine values
to suggest the obvious
kind of crumpling
an eloquent instance
forthcoming from Yale

Proposal in fragments
the initial 'A'
lasted 50 years
towards citation
fortitude and wastage
played out on a terrace
acoustic recording
which he believes
the provenance of
spatial analogies
sufficiently evident
seeks to portray
prosodic contraction
writing to Margaret
down this uneasy

Non-visual quality
of certain ideas
in the background
serves to obscure
letters and telegrams
to secret places
of watery compassion
money experiment
ambiguously gendered
can be related
some figurative sense
seems more interested
in allied air raids
becoming molecular
immediate source

Matter no longer
the overall structure
a strong affinity
never before used
two different forms
counter abstraction
over the precipice
this long summer
multiple displacements
produce an affect
in the early morning
mines closed down
handwritten numbers
opens in chaos
less even than

Nor is nostalgia
an echo chamber
root or sincerity
a near success
along with her sister
the decompression
London's first nightclub
absorbs the latent
warrior ethos
impressionist music
channelled or constrained
a hardworking printer
in dialogue with
a mythical city
refuses to go down

Met at the salon
invented new genres
of human relations
more orderly than
the name of beauty
to be entangled
in what exists
voices and events
after *Gunslinger*
the ice cream social
did not focus
a grammar of presence
as it emerges
lingering uncertainty
released from the cage

Down this uneasy
zero degree
consecutive sequence
decided to cut
various perceptions
torn out of context
rhythmic and vocal
the infinite column
whose paradigm is
desire for an ending
more simply put
and attributed to
the dazzling surface
whatever it is
of urban modernity

Nothing more than
original evidence
is the reader encouraged
to be qualified
and inconsistent
surrealist airiness
transmuted by
resolve and daring
preconceived ethics
a happy memory
using everything
for musical value
would probably say
radical fascism
is mostly quotation

Sixteen at Six times Three

We're done driving to Great Barrington
failing to follow Melville and Thoreau
up the ski-lift mountain slopes

Or boulder-strewn paths in forests.
Think of what haunts you now
but only if you remember: vodka

Amherst, Stockbridge, speeding on the parkway,
meanwhile reconstitute that yeast or year
according to the latest vocational material.

Skim off any foam, reduce the
scattering of finely-sliced spring onions
a sprightly sum, an invincible website

Or a random access Webster's Dictionary.
Underneath the trees and falling leaves
the birds seem to whisper 'Denise'.

Father worked in his own factory
a chance to watch these craftspeople:
consommé, one big dash *Worcestershire* sauce.

Having been to visit Emily Dickinson
in a hired metallic-green mohawk
we shared information with red havoc

That was unspeakable, printed in fascicles,
then sowed herbs in a corner
and came back to tell all:

Some *Tabasco*, lemon, salt and pepper.
I heard a fly buzz, anachronistically,
just before we hit the windshield

And dreamed we might get by
holding onto a wingèd horse
flying high over the hard shoulder.

We'd maybe arrange an export deal
or a Queen's award for anxiety
funnelling forgotten works into translation software.

Sunday brunch needs heaps of dishes.
I heard a bee fizz wickedly
more than I care to remember

Underneath the rocks and falling tortillas.
We're done driving to nonsense county
and back again, AB to Zee:

Benveniste, Betjeman, Bunting,
yellow Auden, blue Yeats, Scarlet O'Hara,
we'd have to end on Zukofsky.

Even with the chorus singing endlessly,
even with the flashbacks flashing back,
we've done derivative in Great Barrington.

Let's imagine this as lyric finality
'How nice to *see* you, Rodefer,'
my vocabulary did this to me.

The Chief

The son of the chief is now chief
a wireless-enabled Van Morrison fan
says that his father sends us greetings,
investment opportunities,
little glass beads,
powder-blue terminator corn
this is astute, no doubt, and more follows.

We apply glyphosate with conviction,
wishing for agent orange
copyright resistant herbicide
hybridising freely with GM rape
walking for/on water, rotors fly over
dead MacSweeney,
friendship and goodwill on my iPod
Are they gunships?
Where is the truth?
Forgotten your password?
Add to basket?
Do you want to save your changes?

We know he has little need of our friendship
when salmon swim northward in warming sea
go to Ayrshire see basking sharks
sand eels in the shallows
zooplankton intellectual property
foil-wrapped glaciers reject the sun,
and turn again: [your username]
metal gathers on the surface
engines speak together on tarmac
burnt fuel spreads out in the sky.

His people are many
eating up the world and all the poor
stars that shine in the heavens above Hollywood
many are they and huge, chicken sandwich, big mac
all over Round-up—Tumbleweed, the scattering people
on the storm-swept soya farm
for your safety and comfort
the rain forest, the cloud magnet,
the definitive Glastonbury guide,
blue-green fractals everywhere,
but those people no longer
see self-similarity.

The big white warrior
sends us this fine-printed errata slip
the great and good five-letter word
could be 'thief' or 'grief', maybe 'chief',
sends us the word that he wants to buy
some living-dwelling-being place,
tripods and forklifts
maybe 'Heidegger'
poor old Heidegger
key words make it easier to search and pay
stored up and printed, corrected, reprinted, archived
with freehold tenancy for all time
buried here, or burnt and scattered
little stones jumping in the rivers
silt that falls at the turn of a slow repeat
good and bad repeats, echoes
echoes of calls in twilit woods
and in daylight unspotted.
Recordings of this soundscape recovered
darkness sounds or screams unknown

with freehold tenancy of no limit
in this searchable electronic register
what did you say about the lavender?
Was it parcelled up and compressed
into a good fixed-rate interest-only scheme
but is now unwilling to allow us reserve enough:
Kirsty is thinking of biodiversity
which we are known for says Abi
can't get you out of my head, Shelby,
but that should allow capital gain,
equity store or release
in benevolent care for all creatures
to live comfortably and not be first born
not be fire-bombed nor nuked, little man, fat boy
(correct this) indeed appears to be generic
the deed appears generous for the red man
appears no longer.
People living together (blank).
No longer has rights, evident or self-evident
no longer living together but taken apart: reserved
and the offer may be wise, also
for we are no longer
no longer in need of a great country.

There was a time when our people covered the whole land
but we are stumped on the stump, exploded
as the waves of a wind-ruffled sea
might be atomized by this device
what you understand by 'thinking' or 'property' or 'benefit'
in future you will have to make sure you copy
our instrumental language, superior technology
mollusc remains, broken and scattered
under the same wind-ruffled moving body of water.

That sea to which all things
for 'iconic' read 'ironic' formations
generalised figurative language,
thus water in any body
walking on the shell-paved shore or floor.
Your train manager speaking
non-stop through to London Paddington
we are three-percent over the bench mark
but that time has long since passed away
apexplaza.co.uk
I will not mourn our untimely decay
p.181, column 2, third headword: for 'Arta' read 'Artas'
there are two narratives in play, danger
in everyway conflicted and violent
declared incommensurable by no international court
put into conflict in tent city.
Will not mourn our decay, timely or whatever
surrounded by razor wire,
patrolled by tanks and helicopters
nor reproach my pale-face brothers for hastening it
following a slow-running preceding service
with the ghost of Doug Oliver
for we too may have been somewhat to blame.

When our young men see trophies they grow angry
cut off from vital forms that sustain growth
their hearts also are disfigured and turn literal
three goals after the joint venture vehicle
[contact Jeshma, request custom demo, hear similar talents]
one by one they go up to the penalty spot
their hearts also are disfigured and turn liberal
particularly young professionals who thrive on pressure
permanent, recurrent or merely haphazard

then is their cruelty relentless and knows no bounds.
It was getting a bit late, I texted her
on the other hand we knew something had happened—
they go figure their faces with black paint
before the penalty shoot-out
she was in a happy state looking forward to her life
but slipped up on the actual lease length.

A *Priori* also treats melancholia, anxiety, eating disorders
when our old men are not able to restore them
images shrink to fit and are posed by models
to protect patients and victims from themselves.

Murderers will receive automatic life sentences no longer:
Serbians, Bosnians, Croatians, Abenaki, Kurds, Apachee,
Kosovans, Montenegrins, Iraqis, Arapaho, Iranians, Scots,
Blackfeet, Vikings, English, Caddo, Canada, Syrians, Azerbaijanis,
Cherokee, Pale-face brothers, French, Vietcong, Chicasaw, Dutch,
Italians, Chippewa, Germans, Ethiopians, Choctaw, Hutus,
Cambodians, Comanche, Angolans, Andersons, Tamils, Creek,
Eritreans, Macleods, Congolese, Delaware, Sudanese, Stevensons,
Welsh, Illinois, Cornish, Tutsis, Iowas, Senegalese, Kansas, Sierra
Leoneans, Kaskakia, Simsiams, Kickapoo, Haidas, Halls, Kiowa,
Massasoit, Burundians, Miami, Nigerians, Mississippi Choctaw,
Missouri, Maravian, Munsee, Mayans, Tibetans, Nepalese,
Croggons, Omaha, Bhutanese, Oneida, Portuguese, Osage,
Ossipee, Otoe, Ottawa, Pawnee, Pequawet, Pottawatomie, Qyap,
Sauk, Seminole, Shawnee, Sioux, Sokoki, Wampanoag, Wyandot,
but what of hostilities between the young men and the old men,
the young women and the old women, the old men and the new
men, the new women and the old women, the frogs and newts,
the squirrels and foxes, the lions and antelopes, the zebras and
cheetahs, the boat race and the road race, the marathon and

stay-at-home, the wide-open beavers, the night-clubbers and high-diners, the tv recliners, the Oggsford Martians and the blood-pudding A-listers, the Avon-calling tutors, the patter jockeys, the down-under dogs, the YBA scribblers, the new new poetry review-ers, the snooty Ambient Baxters, the crinny minimalists and rural relocators, the foxy hunters and the Tory punters, the re-birchers and honey mooners, the minty-bum finalists, the mute bassoon-ers, the self-published narcissists, Otis Johnson himself, the foiled trashcans, the salty dogs, the barker's biscuit, the Alfred Davids, the equidistant pagers, the on-message menacers, the naked ambitions, the Judith E Wilson Alumni, the young fuckers, the Adornettes, the feminist suicides' fan club, the all-comers and outsiders alliance, all have everything to gain and nothing to lose or is it the other way round?

The Estuary Oliver
For Douglas Oliver

Going in through a broken window
an outmoded model of shared knowledge,
still thinking in six-word clusters:
'I was like, "That's all right."'

A speech-bubble in space-time
an island is all the world.
CCTV IN OPERATION: go ahead Doug
tell me what you see there

Up there with the radio voices,
very small moments of self-experience —
some kind of remote blue interior,
moving titles in red LCD flicker

As middle-England unrolls at speed
through guilty embankments full of premonition
using a precise seemingly-traditional form.
A head up over the reeds

Watching harriers when no religious belief
or providential afterlife in ocean blue —
sailing your little boat from Brightlingsea
riding my new MZ with you

Out across the spooky Essex marshes.
Segments of variable revenue moving ahead:
broken messages, psoriasis itch, burnt chicken,
the cheap red velour of breakfast.

This cues a machine-generated voice
mixing blank gable ends with Dutch.
The soundscape includes a running diesel
stopped by the M5, near Taunton.

Let's call it 'Picture Emphasizing Stillness',
two bright red lights the signal
for the end of the line:
a photo-enlarged back-lit croissant.

Not quite turning into the past,
estimated delay is modified and restated:
the gone-dead are beamish and
drowned in a medium green liquid.

The diagonal is surely still diagonal
and the drowned man's voice whooshes
into sounds that want to be
sailing a dinghy beyond point clear.

So go ahead Dr Oliver, inventor.

Title Goes Here

The voice on the tape matched other recordings
but I'm not allowed to

Passed on through blood
story lines we let go

Other moving trains and potential hazards
any fainting fits or turns?

Listen to the drowsy background hum
we don't have a body yet

In the fog of partisan rhetoric
doing a job

We try to listen to what customers want
because, unlike many companies

With a high degree of confidence
causes distress to the victim

They say he/she has a strong personality
and will be taken to pieces

Work them hard. See you later
midway through the first half

Both legs at each press conference
absolutely helpless

Before leaving the train, be aware
Yeah, Yeah, whatever

Which would fully reflect the principle of consent
subjects in photographs

With haemophilia and other bleeding
they're moving about too much

Weapons were merely a deterrent
makes the tongue swell

Based on a fake postcard of Theresienstadt
Abu Ghraib photoshop (your name here)

I want to talk about the setup
the introduction of plot elements

'We all stand in solidarity', Mr Bush said,
moving out of Chippenham

Filmed by his wife during a skiing holiday
shot several times

A captured message
beheaded on videotape

Specific stories, central locking
stains on the walls

Unfolding

Strangers are no longer entirely strangers
warm and still to be enjoy'd
having preserved as far as possible
proportionate and professional use of force
and thus forgo all that ensues
mondegreen powder on a little table
many other calls on your time
She speaks good English and invites
almost to the brim where possible
accused the UN of provoking violence
Before and After the Spanish Conquest
but perhaps the causality does not
(people are sleepy in this novel)
guarantee a full and immediate refund

The beach where I learnt to
protected from financial failure of clients
always replace the cap after use
Christopher will be at his studio
I didn't hit speed redial, but
we can't operate in a vacuum
has been looted by subsequent armies
without even her handbag, only the
feeling of helplessness remained. When you
hid in trees behind the houses
as they amputated the arms of
a skunk walks along the pavement
major channels may still seem reluctant
a creamy way to make a living

Really I don't use any paint
in the Miles river, for lunch
my art is about life right now
intravenous bags which contain various dyes
once I got the electrical cable
and had to borrow a camera
to help poor people you understand
my work has nothing to do
with flood victims, the two images
'Bob' is a flesh coloured foot
these adventures always begin with xeroxes
the startled little waves that leap
I'd send the government a menu
tomato would be very very expensive

Isiah Berlin as a boy from
with no central authority or location
the 'True Blonde at Home' series
voices in the stairwell are not
holding a small gun and influential
designed to be used by strangers
those who are navigating between identities
a social landscape will return shortly
the person has two additional faces
do you ever have that feeling?
they are essays without concluding paragraphs
or intrusion then on my part
the patio in 1913. Later from
her darkest colour is hot pink

As if it was a submarine
in chocolate for no obvious reason
and goes down all at once
because you're bringing home the carpet
those little waves on a pond
neat wrapped in greaseproof paper thus
and the long-held following silence
of a once favourite grey jacket
the shape left by a hazelnut
without an engine. Now I remember
also the images themselves gaining momentum
a loose thread in the sleeve
on the common one fine day
just like a paper boat, floating

Between English bay and the hotel
before they find the exit and
mostly Berrigan's *Sonnets* (1964), but also
including the name of an animal
As is usual, was about over
the system is probably unintelligible now
lined up in the stadium, shot
wearing blue checks was more effective
a fully-working model of everything
to feign what one doesn't have
I know they were all dead
wearing dirty blue checks, regular money
lived in a tent at Germoe
our connection to the Ottawa aristocracy

Rather than being a formal interpretation
Ruskin, Turner and the Pre-Raphaelites
however, shapes the emergence of language
not anchored in the reference field
deliberately vast in scope, so that
these technological erosions of self-sufficiency
sponsored by SUN LIFE PROVINCIAL HOLDINGS
belong to percept: customer not present
The final amount payable will be
deliberately vast in scope, so that
a capital letter loaned out at
fast recovery rate—three to seven
inhabits this gloss, whether or not
touched with comedy and the supernatural

Over a period of five years
one pupil left via the window
white stars topped his rosy snout
I must live in my lanthorn
sift the contents and rinse well
short-term winners in the abstract
a wide range of obscure practices
ink, pencil, crayon, paper, fabric, newspaper,
printed reproductions, painted paper on canvas
do you talk to the spirits?
please list your duties and responsibilities
feel free to come along at
I heard a fly buzz, then
it crashed into the window pane

Rivers and bay, which sparkled so
our generous upgrade for the weekend
of wedding cakes from Latino bakeries
uses the principle of Feng Shui
so it will be like getting
printed with images of raw meat
much enlarged in yellow cast rubber
for car and driver one way
But can painting and drawing convey
a tape, our own little guide
down the front of his robe
'This is your house,' Jeanie said
downstairs to a small exercise room
spilled out of the vehicle, laughing

You will avoid the tiresome business
about 90 slides in a second-hand
I could expand the tree. People
to build and maintain a framework
using car number plates, dress, dates
from one of these worlds. To
living people unconnected with each other
such proofs were possible is rooted
I sought to avoid in mine
and they sold me this package
over a period of five years
the idea was to eliminate variables
the darkest colour is hot pink
Your subscription is due for renewal

No other states in the north east
either call your doctor right away
then peeling off double-sided sheets
the idea was to eliminate vegetables
but since I had the stroke
with rows of unreadable red dots
the poor drowned woman stands in
and older drivers need more light
A luxuriant paranoia spanning East river
using the blue company logo and
unexpectedly the evening caught fire then
whose true sensitivity was camouflaged in
Bits of dialogue are filtered through
in bad or little-seen movies

Additional cover has an overall limit
ridged and brown elm leaves unfold
by referring backwards to source texts
a hydraulic system pumping out sap
the pressure of a running schedule
scholarship, opinions, imagination, struggles and triumphs
displayed on each double-page spread
it's not actually raining right now
the remainder of this ingenious paper
is rooted in proofs such as
simulation of physical reality is expensive
over the whole period, rather than
designed to be used by strangers
for almost seven hours a day

A bomb on Hammersmith bridge explodes
they kiss. Zap! They leave me
a couple of hours but I
have a safety chain. Alaric dead—
Warhol's brushwork. No more local bonfires
on a diet of broken biscuits
set in motion but not controlled
didn't I have you once for
everything hung on the rigs must
the distance from Blackfriars to Waterloo
words that do ring truly banal
we wrapped money in this paper
wood fell onto the kitchen floor
what do you mean legitimation crisis?

Assuming this to be the real
and even below the gum line
much of the letter is true
if you have a history of
what does 'bad confessionalism' mean exactly?
everyone who filled in the questionnaire
is in any way autobiographical, and
say farewell to our long tradition
of picture cards. TANGY YELLOW BISCUIT
forward to some exciting new ideas
DO NOT TAKE HALF-INDERAL LA
we do it all the time
the strong glare of Keats' career
use by see end of tube

Assume everyone knows this is anywhere
that you might care to be
and there glimpse an illegible world
back-lit images of obscure letters
will the fragile manuscript be left
up into her room? Hello Kev.
set in peaceful tropical gardens, before
breaking this seal or using software
recap after use. SOCIAL EXCLUSION UNIT
that would have him not be
like talking to the Women's Institute
from a window: bay, yew, oak
three kinds of green but no
There are other indications of inconsistency

A bus on London bridge ignites
they fall. Nothing! They go down
a couple of floors but I
have a new policy. Douglas dead
Uglow's brushwork. Who was that masked . . .
on a diet of rigs must
preserved in resin but not controlled
Didn't I do this one already?
so much depends on broken biscuits
the distance from Putney to Wimbledon
words that do feelings, really sublime!
They wrapped paper in this money
sawdust fell on the bathroom floor
what do you mean transcendent longing?

Took our coffee out onto the
warm and hospitable as she was
bordered by Moorish geometries. But is
notable for the mingled expression of
silver gilt with applied enamels, attributed
really a unicorn with human feet
having not been displayed or exhibited
shall be an insured person while
to which this group policy relates
We get lucky and things work
rack of lamb with pistachio and
love to see a bluebird', said
from which the patio was stripped
at the time of such disappearance

Or even to make single images
generic front runners did not participate
in the context of popular culture
to turn off the marked road
after alighting from such an aircraft
the first night, doling out upgrades
between the point of departure and
such injury received while riding as
the watchman falls into the trap.
In a 1992 catalogue essay, falling
or alighting from, or being struck
will be paid if specified below.
A bomb on Hammersmith bridge explodes
the greatest sorrow I ever knew

Z Screen

From the forces of nature. These are 'mechanical birds'
hanging from a chandelier as if they had abolished
all literal meaning. The brain has become a blur
in the discourse of painting and is mostly fat.
Table 5 adds to this dichotomy
but no-one imagined she was a saint. Spot colour blue,
reads alert but neutral. The barbed wire looks like foliage.
You run around and shoot at cars viewed from above,
patched-in sirens and packets of crash soundtrack.
People from care homes in TV's next big reality show
called *Collateral Damage*. In rapid expansion
the dust clouds perfectly demonstrate self-similarity,
neglecting home viewers. Most innovators go bust.
Foliage partly hides a waiting tank that slowly turns.
The diary holds within it an implied criticism
worked out in diffuse landscape remnants
with plenty of chrome. Turbines or radiators
bring him back into focus by late afternoon
as the linseed evaporates. Pyres are still burning
coal, pallets, and straw piled up in the fields, ready to go.